Surprising Facts About Being a

MARINE

by Kristin J. Russo

Consultant:
Kurt Waeschle, Chief of Operations
Navy Region Northwest Fire and Emergency Services

CAPSTONE PRESS
a capstone imprint

Edge Books are published by Capstone Press,
1710 Roe Crest Drive, North Mankato, Minnesota 56003
www.mycapstone.com

Library of Congress Cataloging-in-Publication Data
Names: Russo, Kristin J., author.
Title: Surprising facts about being a Marine / by Kristin J Russo.
Description: North Mankato, Minnesota : Capstone Press, [2018] | Series: Edge
  books. What you didn't know about the U.S. military life | Includes
  bibliographical references and index. | Audience: Grades 4-6. |
Audience: Ages 8-14.
Identifiers: LCCN 2017008350| ISBN 9781515774273 (library binding) | ISBN 9781515774310 (ebook pdf)
Subjects: LCSH: United States. Marine Corps--Juvenile literature. |
  Marines--United States--Juvenile literature.
Classification: LCC VE23 .R89 2018 | DDC 359.9/60973--dc23
LC record available at https://lccn.loc.gov/2017008350

Editorial Credits
Nikki Ramsay, editor; Sara Radka, designer; Laura Manthe, production specialist

Photo Credits
Getty Images: Chip Somodevilla, 9, David McNew, 12, 15, Dondi Tawatao, 22, Lance Cpl. David N. Hersey/U.S.
Marines, 21, Matt Cardy, 16, Matthew Cavanaugh, 23, Michael Q. Retana, 29, Rubberball, 6, Scott Olson, 7,
Stocktrek Images, 19, Ted Banks/U.S. Navy, 20, U.S. Navy, 18; Newscom: DoD/Sipa USA, 17, U.S. Marine Corps/
Sipa USA, 8, ZUMAPRESS/Cpl. Henry Antenor/Planet Pix, 25, Newscom, ZUMAPRESS/Lcpl. Christopher
A. Mendoza/Planet Pix, 27, ZUMAPRESS/Max Blumenfeld/Planet Pix, 24, ZUMAPRESS/Mcs1 Shannon E.
Renfroe/Planet Pix, 28, ZUMAPRESS/Paul Peterson/Planet Pix, 4, ZUMAPRESS/Sgt. Christopher Q. Stone, cover;
Wikimedia: Lance Cpl. Christopher Mendoza, 26, U.S. Navy/Photographer's Mate 1st Class Shane T. McCoy, 13,
U.S.M.C., 11

Graphic elements by Book Buddy Media.

Printed in the United States of America.
010364F17

TABLE OF CONTENTS

RUNNING TOWARD CHAOS

Most people would not like to be called a "leatherneck." But to a U.S. Marine, the name is a sign of respect. Long ago Marines used to wear leather straps around their necks to avoid being stabbed by a pirate's sword. This is where people think the nickname came from.

Today the Marine Corps is part of the U.S. Navy, but it has its own specific purpose. Marines are sent in first when a war that involves the United States breaks out. Marines can give the most amount of help in the shortest amount of time. They are trained to "run toward **chaos**." They move quickly by air, land, and sea to solve problems around the globe.

You may know that Marines go through a difficult boot camp, which tests their physical limits. They then go through more training related specifically to the jobs they will do. But do you know why Marines must train so hard? Some rush toward bombs to dispose of them before they explode. Others inject fuel into a helicopter while it is still running. Get ready to learn even more amazing facts that will open your eyes to what it's like to be a Marine.

chaos—complete disorder and confusion

Sliding down a thick cable from a hovering helicopter is called "fast-roping." Marines do not always use a safety harness when they fast-rope, and this can be dangerous if they fall.

Chapter 1

BECOMING A MARINE

ENLIST

The Marine Corps motto is *Semper Fidelis*. It means "always faithful" in Latin. Marines take their motto seriously. They are always loyal to their country and to one another.

Becoming a Marine is not easy. The training is challenging. **Recruits** must be at least 17 years old. They must also have a

Combat Fitness

The combat fitness test is the same for men and women. Recruits must run an 880-yard (804-meter) sprint in heavy combat uniforms. They lift 30 pounds (13.6 kilograms) of ammunition over their heads as many times as they can. They must also move quickly through an obstacle course to show **agility**.

Strength and Physical Fitness

Both men and women must prove that they are strong enough to serve as Marines. Men must be able to do pull-ups and women must do a flexed-arm hang. Recruits must also be able to do several crunches in one minute and run 1.5 miles (2.4 kilometers) in a timed run.

recruit—a person newly enlisted in the armed forces and not yet fully trained

agility—the ability to move swiftly and nimbly

Recruits train to survive in the water while wearing all of their combat gear. This can include a rifle, helmet, bulletproof jacket, and pack.

FACT The Marines' first battle took place on March 4, 1776, during the American Revolutionary War (1775–1783). About 200 Marines captured the British Fort Nassau in the Bahamas. The Marines took about 100 cannons, 15 mortars, and 11,000 rounds of ammunition. The weaponry was brought back and used by George Washington's Continental Army.

BECOME AN OFFICER

There are a few paths to becoming a Marine officer. Attending the U.S. Naval Academy in Annapolis, Maryland, is one way. Attending the U.S. Marine University at Quantico Base in Virginia is another. **Enlistees** can also apply to the Marine Corps Enlisted Commissioning Education Program (MECEP). MECEP offers enlisted Marines the chance to go to a four-year college full-time while they remain on active duty. They would then be able to go to Officer Candidate School (OCS)

enlistee—a person who has joined or signed up

U.S. Naval Academy

Students who go to the Naval Academy can also become Marine officers when they graduate. Students in their third year at the Naval Academy can attend what is called leatherneck training. Leatherneck training is a four-week summer program. Marines operate in smaller units than other branches of the military. That is why training focuses on small-unit leadership. This can be hard for some recruits who must learn to give and take orders from people who have become their friends.

Officer Candidate School

Students who attend any college can apply to OCS at Quantico Base in Virginia. They attend during the summer and learn combat and decision-making skills. They also learn how to handle basic weapons. They can then become Marine officers after they graduate from college.

 **FACT** Officer candidates at OCS must complete the "Tarzan" course. They swing, jump, and climb on a series of ropes and ladders set high off the ground.

Chapter 2

TRAINING

EAST COAST AND WEST COAST

There are two basic training locations for the Marines. All female recruits go to boot camp at Parris Island, South Carolina. Men who live east of the Mississippi River also report to Parris Island for boot camp. All other men go to boot camp in San Diego, California. Men and women live and train in separate quarters at Parris Island. The Marine Corps is the only military branch that separates men and women during training.

The Crucible

All recruits must pass the "Crucible" test to become a Marine. Recruits get only eight hours of sleep and two-and-a-half MREs (Meals, Ready-to-Eat) during the 54-hour exercise. They must measure out their food. They march about 40 miles (64 km) and do a night **infiltration** course. The night course is difficult. Recruits must climb under barbed wire with flares and **simulated** gunfire flying overhead.

Boot Camp for Women

All men and women in infantry and combat jobs must meet the same tough standards. The first female infantry Marines graduated boot camp in January of 2017.

Sound Like a Marine

Recruits learn new vocabulary at boot camp. They use **nautical** terms. In the Marines, the floor is a "deck." The walls are "bulkheads." Windows are "portholes." When they go upstairs, they go "topside."

Recruits who forget to use this new way of speaking could be "quarter decked." This means they do a fast-paced series of exercises. Marines could be told to run in place and complete a certain number of push-ups.

The Crucible helps recruits rely on their fellow Marines. It also builds self-reliance and confidence.

FACT Some drill instructors yell at recruits so loudly and for so long that they pass out, which can happen when not enough oxygen reaches their brains. Yelling can also damage their vocal chords. Drill instructors receive special training to prevent permanent problems from all the yelling they do.

infiltration—the action of entering or gaining access to an organization or place secretly, especially in order to acquire secret information or cause damage

simulated—pretend

nautical—of or concerning sailors and ships

MILITARY OCCUPATIONAL SPECIALTY TRAINING

After boot camp, Marines move on to job training. Jobs are called Military Occupational Specialties (MOSs). There are about 180 possible MOSs for enlistees in more than 35 different fields. Most are combat related, but some involve other tasks.

The length of each MOS school varies. It can be four weeks or more than a year. The length of training depends on the job. Electrical repair MOSs require training that can last from 10 to 50 weeks. Some vehicle and machinery mechanic MOSs can take from 6 to 18 weeks to complete.

Infantry units train to deal with extreme weather at the Marine Corps Air Ground Combat Center near the Mojave Desert in California. Summer high temperatures are above 100 degrees Fahrenheit (37 degrees Celsius) and in the winter get down to 20°F (minus 7°C).

Choosing an MOS

Recruits like to choose their MOS before they go to boot camp. They will not always be allowed their first choice. How they perform at boot camp will decide if they can be posted to their favorite MOS. The Marine enlistees must take a test called the Armed Services Vocational Battery. Enlistees in all U.S. military branches must take this test. A high score on this test allows enlistees the most job options.

Unusual Career Paths

Most jobs in the Marines have something to do with combat. But the jobs that are not combat-related are still very important. Some Marines train in different languages and serve as interpreters and translators. They help interview friendly locals in their native language. They help **interrogate** enemies.

Lawyers are also needed in the Marines. They are called judge advocates. They try criminal cases and give legal advice. They also advise battlefield commanders about international law and the rules of warfare.

Marines may be responsible for directing civilians passing through checkpoints in foreign countries.

FACT The first woman to serve as a Marine was Lucy Brewer. She pretended to be male and used the name George Baker to serve on board the ship USS *Constitution* in 1812.

interrogate—to ask questions aggressively of someone, especially a suspect or a prisoner

Chapter 3

MARINE AIR-GROUND TASK FORCES

Marine Air-Ground Task Forces (MAGTFs) are designed to respond to a crisis quickly anywhere in the world. They sometimes respond in only six hours after receiving notification. There are different types of task forces, including the Marine Expeditionary Force, the Marine Expeditionary Brigade, and the Marine Expeditionary Unit. MAGTFs have four elements: Ground Operations, Aviation, Logistics, and Command.

GROUND OPERATIONS

The Ground Operations Combat Element fills many roles when it comes to ground combat. Some, such as cannoneers, are in charge of weapons. Others, such as **intelligence** officers, look for secret information that will help combat troops. Only ground operation specialists are allowed to take control of and **occupy** an area of land.

Ground Intelligence

Ground intelligence officers observe and collect information about weather and terrain. They also report on the location of enemy soldiers. They create maps that show safe and unsafe areas in enemy territory. Ground **operatives** use this information to make **tactical** decisions about where to go and what to do in combat situations. Commanders use this information to plan and carry out combat or rescue missions.

intelligence—the collection of information of military value by observation and reconnaissance

occupy—to take and keep control of by using military power

Operatives in the Logistics Combat Element make sure Marines have everything they need on a mission, including computers and communication devices, even in remote or mountainous areas.

FACT The smallest type of MAGTF is the Marine Expeditionary Unit (MEU). There are about 2,200 Marines in an MEU. The largest type of MAGTF is the Marine Expeditionary Brigade (MEB). There are about 14,500 Marines in an MEB.

operative—a person who works toward achieving the objectives of a larger interest

tactical—for use in immediate support of military or naval operations

AVIATION

The second part of a MAGTF unit is the Aviation Combat Element. Aviation teams are stationed near troubled areas around the globe. They are always close to where they are needed so that they can respond quickly. When help is needed, the aviation team reviews weather and flight plans and organizes a response. The Aviation Combat Element is organized into groups of at least 500 members. These groups fly and service at least 25 to 30 different types of aircraft.

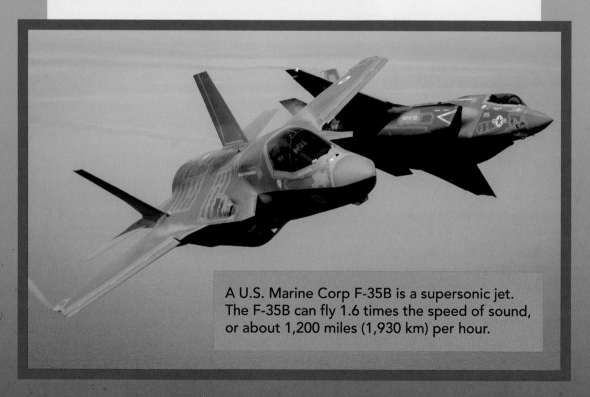

A U.S. Marine Corp F-35B is a supersonic jet. The F-35B can fly 1.6 times the speed of sound, or about 1,200 miles (1,930 km) per hour.

Pilots

Becoming a Marine pilot is not easy. Pilots must have at least a bachelor's degree from any college or military university. Training includes hundreds of hours of instruction in aviation and navigation. Instruction on land and sea survival is also needed. Marine pilots fly fixed-wing planes, supersonic fighter jets, and a variety of helicopters.

Air Intelligence

Air intelligence officers gather information so that pilots can make combat decisions in the air. Air intelligence officers need to have excellent computer and communications skills in order to understand and share important information.

Small, unmanned drones such as the RQ-11B Raven are used to gather information about the land. They can fly for up to 90 minutes and can take pictures at night.

It is the aviation crew's job to complete hot refueling of military helicopters.

Aircraft Refuelers

Some aviation crew members take care of airplanes rather than fly them. Their jobs can be just as dangerous as the pilots' jobs. Aviation crews do what is called "hot refueling." This is done when a helicopter needs to be refueled in a short amount of time. This means they put jet fuel into the aircraft while it is still running. It takes four refuelers to make sure the helicopter does not roll over. Also, a grounding wire is attached to keep static electricity from setting the jet fuel on fire.

LOGISTICS

Marines cannot work without the right equipment and tools. The third part of the MAGTF unit — the Logistics Combat Element — helps the unit move quickly with the equipment that they need to complete the mission. Each Logistics Combat Element is made up of about 300 Marines.

EOD technicians are trained to detonate bombs without destroying the surrounding area.

Explosive Ordnance Disposal

Some logistics team members take on the hazardous role of Explosive **Ordnance** Disposal Technician. EOD technicians are a very important part of the logistics team. The EOD team is called when a device is found that could be a bomb. Members are trained to take apart or detonate many different types of bombs safely. The training also includes dealing with both chemical and **nuclear weapons**. Sometimes they use robots that can do the work remotely. EOD technicians clear any obstacle that keeps the MAGTF from completing its mission. This could include unexploded rockets or land mines.

ordnance—military supplies such as weapons or ammunition

nuclear weapon—a powerful weapon that can destroy a large area

Marines are trained to airlift supplies to areas that can't be reached by other methods.

Humanitarian Relief

Marines provide **humanitarian** help to those hurt by storms and other disasters all around the world. The Logistics Combat Element plays an important role in bringing food and water to places cut off from supplies. Marines also deliver medical help where needed.

Disaster can strike anywhere and at any time. Marines are trained to respond with humanitarian relief at a moment's notice. One training area where Marines practice relief exercises is in Queensland, Australia.

humanitarian—concerned with or seeking to promote human welfare

Supply Administration

An aviation crew member needs a special part to repair a helicopter. A Marine has a damaged uniform and needs a replacement. A pilot sees that an aircraft is low on fuel. It is the supply administrator's job to track down these items and make sure they are available to all members of the MAGTF team. Without supply administrators, Marines would not have the things that they need to get the job done.

COMMAND

The final piece of the MAGTF is the Command Combat Element. Though there is only one commander who acts as a leader on missions, there are about 200 members of the combat element. Mostly, Marines who serve in the Command Combat Element collect and share information.

The commander collects information from all elements of the MAGTF and uses it to make decisions to plan and carry out missions. Commanders lead in many different kinds of operations, including combat and disaster relief.

It is the Public Affairs Officer's job to answer questions from the media. The public can learn about combat missions or other events as long as the information is not classified, or secret.

Public Affairs Officers

The Command Combat Element of a MAGTF includes a public affairs officer. Public affairs officers study important topics and share that information. They answer questions and write articles about what is happening in the Marine Corps. If you wanted to know when a unit of **deployed** Marines was coming home, you would ask a Public Affairs Officer.

Cyber-Electronic Warfare Center

The Cyber-Electronic Warfare Center is made up of Marines serving in the Command Combat Element. These cyber warriors learn new tactics and techniques to gain information found in computer networks and the Internet. They share this information with the MAGTF commander. It can be used to protect U.S. computer networks from a cyberattack.

deploy—to move troops or equipment into position for military action

Chapter 4

ELITE FORCES

ORIGIN OF "RAIDERS"

The Marines special forces unit used to be known as the Marine Corps Forces Special Operations Command (MARSOC). In 2015 the Marines in MARSOC received a new name. Their name became the Raiders. This new name honors a group of soldiers that took risky assignments during World War II (1939–1945).

First to Respond

There are only 2,700 to 3,000 Raiders in total. The Raiders are highly trained. They are often called in first when a conflict or emergency strikes. They support both U.S. and foreign soldiers trying to fight the threat of terrorism around the world.

A Marine never goes anywhere without a buddy. The two Marines protect each other.

WHO BECOMES A RAIDER?

Before becoming a Raider, candidates participate in a 23-day selection program. It begins at Camp Lejeune in North Carolina. Candidates run 8 to 10 miles (13 to 16 km) and lift heavy weights. They swim in their uniforms. They tread water for 11 minutes and then float for 4 minutes using their shirts or pants. Candidates who complete the first phase are moved to an unknown location for more exercises and mental fitness training.

The program is so difficult that some candidates are tempted to quit. Candidates are encouraged to mentally commit to the challenge before it starts. This will make them more likely to succeed. A common Marines saying is, "Never make a decision while you're going uphill."

In a "hard duck," Marines are dropped into the water from a helicopter in a fully inflated rubber boat.

Marines train to survive in the water with their hands and feet bound. They learn to swim like dolphins, kicking with their feet together to reach the surface.

Raiders Training

Raiders are well trained in combat skills. They train to drive aggressively and survive when their vehicle rolls over. They also learn to shoot a gun or rifle accurately under stress. Marines usually have only a quarter of a second to find a target and squeeze the trigger while in combat. Raiders are trained for this and other high-stress combat situations.

WORKING WITH ALL MILITARY BRANCHES

Marines train to work in the air, on the ground, and on the sea. This makes them valuable to all of the branches of the U.S. military. The Army, Navy, and Air Force rely on Marine units for leadership and support in times of trouble.

An amphibious assault vehicle can hold 21 Marines. It can launch grenades while in the ocean or on land.

Working with the Army

Marines and Army soldiers train together so that they will be ready to serve together in the field. In one shared exercise, Marine helicopters place two **howitzers** in an open field. Army soldiers prepare, fire, and remove the weapons in only 45 minutes. The Marines and the Army learn to work together so that real-life combat events will be successful.

Working with the Navy

Marines also train and work with Navy sailors. Marines work with Navy sailors to drive assault vehicles that can go in both land and water. These vehicles leave Navy assault ships, move in the water, and transport Marines to and through unsafe areas. They carry Marines and supplies to support combat troops on the battlefield. The Marines provide security on Navy ships as well.

howitzer—a cannon that shoots explosive shells long distances

GLOSSARY

agility (uh-GI-luh-tee)—the ability to move swiftly and nimbly

chaos (KAY-os)—complete disorder and confusion

deploy (di-PLOY)—to move troops or equipment into position for military action

enlistee (in-LIST-ee)—a person who has joined or signed up

howitzer (HOW-it-zer)—a cannon that shoots explosive shells long distances

humanitarian (hyoo-man-uh-TAIR-ee-uhn)—concerned with or seeking to promote human welfare

infiltration (in-fil-TRAY-shun)—the action of entering or gaining access to an organization or place secretly, especially in order to acquire secret information or cause damage

intelligence (in-TEL-uh-jenss)—the collection of information of military value by observation and reconnaissance

interrogate (in-TER-uh-gate)—to ask questions aggressively of someone, especially a suspect or a prisoner

nautical (NAW-tuh-kuhl)—of or concerning sailors and ships

nuclear weapon (NOO-klee-ur WEP-uhn)—a powerful weapon that can destroy a large area

operative (OP-er-a-tiv)—a person who works toward achieving the objectives of a larger interest

ordnance (ORD-nanss)—military supplies such as weapons or ammunition

recruit (ri-KROOT)—a person newly enlisted in the armed forces and not yet fully trained

tactical (TAK-ti-kuhl)—for use in immediate support of military or naval operations

READ MORE

Bozzo, Linda. *Marine Expeditionary Units.* Serving in the Military. Mankato, Minn.: Amicus High Interest, 2015.

Doeden, Matt. *Can You Survive in the Special Forces?: An Interactive Survival Adventure.* You Choose: Survival. Mankato, Minn.: Capstone Press, 2013.

Raum, Elizabeth. *U.S. Marines by the Numbers.* Military by the Numbers. North Mankato, Minn.: Capstone Press, 2014.

INTERNET SITES

Use FactHound to find Internet sites related to this book.

Visit *www.facthound.com*

Just type in 9781515774273 and go.

INDEX